Also by

Rosa Nadine Xochimilco Sánchez

Hearts Aflame, Still Burning

Available in Print and Kindle Editions

ROSA NADINE XOCHIMILCO SÁNCHEZ

Blue Bones

Blood Roses

Black Eyes

Poems by

ROSA NADINE

XOCHIMILCO SÁNCHEZ

Copyright © Walt Whitman's Birthday 2019

Xochimilco Press

———————————

Cover Image by Rosa Nadine Xochimilco Sánchez

Author Image by Phil Gevaux

Cover Design by Phil Gevaux

All rights reserved.

ISBN: 978-0-578-47586-8

DEDICATION

This one is for:

ALYSHA NADINE COHEN

ANGELA OWENS

MICHELLE DUAH

NICHOLAS RYAN HOWARD

They know about broken bones,
They know about blood and roses,
They know about black eyes and blacker hearts;
They know where the bodies are buried.

Love to them all.

xo

And for Phil, for helping to sew the wounds closed. Love you so.

For those of you that didn't know,
Now you do.

For those of you that have experienced a
similar pain,
Know that you are not alone.

-R

TABLE OF CONTENTS

BLUE BONES, BLOOD ROSES, BLACK EYES

BLUE BONES, BLOOD ROSES, BLACK EYES

I. Blue

ROSA NADINE XOCHIMILCO SÁNCHEZ

1. "Uncharted"

The rain it pounds the ground outside,
The droplets drip the other way;
My tears are lost within the window pane,
Tidal waves of regret,
Washing them away.

Broken hearts and broken limbs,
The trees are bleeding precious sap;
The forest longs of rest and respite,
But the fires are still burning, a never ending trap.

Cool ocean breezes soothe the wounded,
A moment of light amongst the pain;
Uncharted waters form treacherous triangles,
The winds pushing me further into the fray.

I didn't want a life of luxury,
I only wanted truth and respect;
You abandoned me, your home, your life, for
nothing,
It's almost tragic now how you seem so perplexed.

This is the consequence of lying,
Complete failure, this is the path you set;
My love was pawned for cheap thrills and a clear
vinyl umbrella,
Now memories of monsoons and floodplains are all
you have left.

The rain it pounds the ground outside,
The droplets drip the other way;
My tears are lost within the window pane;
Tidal waves of regret washing them away,

I want to remember better times,
But the lies have compounded to make themselves
true;
I used to believe my skin was a canvas,
But I didn't mean for you to paint me black and blue.

The fields of flowers I used to dream of,
Were real and never made for you;
The path I took to find Valhalla,
Required a heart that was pure and true.

Broken hearts and broken limbs,
The trees are bleeding precious sap;

The forest longs for rest and respite,

But the fires are still burning, a never ending trap.

Recovery is made of snowflakes,

Delicate, fragile, and inherently cold;

Alone in a crowd the pain cuts deeply,

Burning yourself in ice, letting numbness take hold.

But even though the storm it rages,

Uprooting lives and lives in rage;

There is the Eye to pray to always,

A welcome welcoming savior, disguising the reality of

its cage.

Cold ocean breezes soothe the wounded,

A moment of light amongst the pain;

Uncharted waters form treacherous triangles,

Rain or shine, I'll never sail this way again.

2. "Nebula Of Thorns"

These tears are made of mercury
They move, I fall, I cry
They fall from all the planets
Bending stars into the sky

I look too long for loneliness
I love to long for you
But all I feel is hollow
It's all I know is true

There has to be some other way
To leave and dream and fly
There has to be some other path
Where I don't want to die

There has to be another way
Some sort of secret plan
But I lost my sense of direction
The moment that you ran

Now you've gone back to your fortress
With all your soldiers at your side

And spun this hell as victory
But no one knows you lied

There isn't anything to do
But find my own way made new
And even though I feel so blind
It's time I left you far behind.

3. "Renaissance"

Your kisses were like whispers
Your silence filled my dreams
You spoke I woke and waited
Still nothing was as it seemed

You told me that
You loved me
But at point of gun and pain

You told me that
You loved me
And soon nothing was the same

A whirlwind of night made day
Frozen fried and melting ice
Enveloped chaos all consuming
Twisting through my life

You told me that
You wanted me
But was nothing but fail safe lies

You told me that

You wanted me

And it turns out to you I was merely a prize

Fallen knights and blackened days

I loved and lived in hope made real

Yet you were just pretending

And in the end you left me

And all I could do was feel

4. "Laid Plain"

Torn and tied
lost in the wilderness
curled and coiffed
my stilettos just sink into the mud

Half of everything
half of nothing
buried and born again
blistered and buttered, ready to serve

Twisting and twirling
there are no white flags
There's just your white skin
while I lay here in rags

There is no right turn
There are no train tracks
There is no window
Walls of mirrors show me only pain

5. "Fortress Enflamed"

Here in the darkness
I cower
Cold

Without you
No light
No Dawn

Enshrouded in Memoirs
Entombed in the museum
Of my old life

I want to burn it all down
Burn it all
Down

6. "Sonnet Of Sadness"

And the tears

they fall so endless

As I cry and die and burn

haunted even by your memory

with every laugh and song and yearn

And still you taunt and elude me

from your pedestal on high

for it's my memory you kill

As you lie and lie and lie

7. "Blindness"

I burned a hole

in my existence

trying to stare

into your soul

my flesh peeling

from the bone in layers

all the while it was me

chasing you

for I could do nothing

but watch you run

cowardice

dipped in egotist

you told me it was

me

saying it was I

who abandoned you

all the while to was me

crying for you

while you did nothing

but try to flee

I cried when I couldn't see
the stars anymore
your fire had eaten
my eyes
the acid tears having
become too much
all the while it was me
dying for you
my body bathing in nothing
but your lies

8. "Parts"

How does it feel to climb over my broken bones?
You play to love or, do you revel in mind?
This ongoing pain as you tear my flesh apart;
Watching your shining face as you continue to break
my heart.

How does it feel to climb over my broken bones?
Are they sharp or smooth; are they rough or torn?
Are they carved into intricate figures - part of my
new indigenous history;
Your pretend past continued conquering man of a
woman
White over Brown has been man over wife.

How does it feel to crawl over my broken bones?
Do you wear them as a suit
Do you show them off to all you know?
No?
Do you pretend I don't exist or do you simply
pretend that you are the hero?
How does it feel to crawling on my broken bones?

Can you feel the shattered heart Beneath?

Or are you too worried about your stubbed toe?

9. "Commute(d)"

wherein I believe in justice

and I believe in truth

there is despair in your deception

your sad cry out for youth

I want to whisper in the windows

I want to worship in your pain

of all your incongruous ideas

but still I can not make you sane

For you are held hostage by your spectres

you are reveling in their chains

you could break free even if you wanted to

but you do not want to change

rapt and rollicking in your sadness

celebrating that which does you depress

I beg of you so sweetly

to lay your head down; let it rest

But you champion your crying

and you champion your choice for despair

But your claims become more childish
like today when someone on the train pulled your
hair

I wish that I could help you
I wish that you could see
but I believe in truth and justice
yet you don't believe in me

10. "Never, Never"

Here in the darkness
I feel the sadness
The regret for the loss
Of the life we once loved.

There in the quiet of the porch light
I remember how I missed you
And how I would listen for your key in the door.

We held hands in the garden
I looked for you there in the darkness of the night.

Your hand was all I had for you had taken your body
away to fly
'Til death do us part; Second Star to the Right.

And I remembered why I missed you
Even though you never left the light on for me when
I was out late.

And I close my eyes and we're dancing
Yet I realize you can't see through

The haze of hate.

Here in the darkness
I feel the sadness
The regret for the loss
Of the life we once loved.

You turn to twirl me awhile longer
Suddenly air born I start to fall away
And my tears fall sideways like rain
Teeny tiny droplets
Pure unfiltered pain.

11. "Rooftops"

I wander whispering
Why did you love me

When did the day become so true
That all falsities overruled

Tell me again how you wanted to love me
How it was my fault that you left

How in the swirl of your insecurity
It was me who was plainly deaf

I wander whispering on the moors
Eager to avoid the road

And I know you're out there somewhere
Making excuses as to why you can't move forward

12. "B Minor"

And there you sit and whisper
And there you are to me
One hundred thousand lonely voices

    Longing for
    someone to be

With every turn and stop on the road
I see you in my mirror
Watching everything on the outside

    Thinking thoughts
    only you can hear

13. "Marriage Past"

I still sit on our couch
Feeling at home.

Even though home is gone;
Gone like you,
Gone like love.

Gone gone away.

This couch feels like home,
and I realize I spent my
time on it alone.

Home was alone.

You just happened to be there.

14. "10,000 Foot Hedge"

For it's here in the dreams of this shadow life
with my broken hearts
and my shadow strife;

Where I strive to behave and believe and blend in
to my own sad death
and then begin again.

I look to emote with the purpose of dreams
but desire is elusive
and my tears run in streams;

It's all hope and plans and signing on the line
until I simply can't bear it
until it's finally my time.

So I wander the maze of worlds made real
and look to long for a purpose
but left with nothing but what I feel.

15. "Enshrouded"

How is it that
time passes
so slowly for you
melting clocks and
folded socks
and pain in balls of dough

why is it that
you haunt me so
making my pain
your life's work
collecting perks while
you're the jerk
and I lay filled with sorrow

16. "Blue Moon"

Where do you go
In the midnight hours
When I'm all alone
With the moon?

No call, no show
Not anywhere
And nowhere
Close to home

I cry out in pain
Across the plain
My womb
Empty and shrill

I'm lost along
This country path
Who knew I'd be
Here this long

Where do you go
In the midnight hours

When I'm all alone
With the moon?

Under the stairs
Your hand in her hair
Far from my
Microwave "Meal for One"

I sigh again
And it echoes
The furniture
All gone

Your memory
Warm in the shadows though
I sit
And pray for dawn

17. "The Poison Is Quick"

Sitting in silence I count
The minutes of my pain
Of that darkened house,
Of the second I went insane

Of peers who pushed me down
And told my tale
But me I was the villain,
A ghost in a veil

I want to turn and cry,
But the tears burn my hands
These are only memories,
Trapped in a jar of sand

I stand corrected now that there is no hope
These lies you told stand
My effigy hangs in memory
From vines of rope entwined

For whoever stands
And chooses to believe,

I am done now,

It's my turn to leave.

18. "Footsteps On The Stairs"

I'm always second, always lesser
Always just behind the throne
Unending succession of your mistress
And still I find myself alone.

Alone in darkness, alone in terror
Alone in shadows, alone in fright
I do not hope for my redemption
Here is my sword, I can't stomach the fight.

Another round begins with no opponent
Curtailed enthusiasm, restricted glee
All your wishing for my disappearance
Has finally come true; I had to flee.

And in the pain of your transgression
You never asked me why it hurt
I was your aggressor, not your victim
For not lifting up my skirt.

Entitled Barons in their castles
Made of cardboard, made of praise

Running through the friends you've made off charity
Your ongoing destruction causing no delays.

I can not contain this simple sadness
I can not pretend I'll be at home
Instead I'll be begging your memory for mercy
To simply go away, leave me alone.

Assassination was no option
Suicide a difference curse
So I remain enslaved to you forever
Under God and everything else far worse.

So keep your doors locked, and your windows
If you value your newest trinkets, your trophy wife,
Because the boogeyman is coming,
I'm coming to for you, to haunt your perfect life.

19. "Moses Knew"

I had never really understood
Why adultery was one
Of the ten
Commandments

But much like murder
It is about death
The soul is mortally wounded

In those days, no medicine
There must have been
A lot
Of
Sudden death
Death from infection
Incurableness

Now there are life saving measures
CPR
Machines to breathe
Feeding tubes

But it is still a mortal wound,

And intensive care is expensive.

20. "Belonging To The Underworld"

I had to pretend
Feign disregard

I had to choose
To mistake attention
For respect

To give up dreams
Of a better place

To refocus my world
So it only covered
2 square blocks

I had to make
An effective

Case
Perpetually
Persuading

Everyone

That I was happy

With my unhappiness

21. "Oz"

So tell me
Friend
Why am I still dwelling
The wounds so slowly
Healing
The putrid guild of
Association
Trying to creep from
The edges of freshly
Grown skin and progress
Sometimes so unconsciously
Lost
In the dearth of
Disappointment
Revealing that
I am only a
Shadow behind
A curtain.

That my real nature is that
Which I deny.

That I am not enough.

22. "Sideshow"

There is no dream in second chances

There is no final kind revue

There are no curtain calls for failures

And there is nothing here for you.

So pack up your sad-eye soliloquy

And your self-important monologue

And stay the fuck away from my family

While I do the same to yours.

I have everything you stand for

All your impatient trying cries

I hate you more and more each winter

I know you see it in my eyes.

So tell me again that you're my better

Tell me again I should bow down

Tell me again to scrape your boots for you

Tell me again this is your town.

And hear me whisper in the distance

And you know I will tell the truth

That I am ruthless in my conviction
And that vengeance is my pleasure when it comes to
you.

And now you sit alone and broken
Another sycophant on the hook
And you tell them I'm the devil
But to that I say, "Yes! Come Here! Have a look!"

For when they see that I am honest
And deception is your cloak
They realize you are vapid and hollow
And that maybe they've misspoke.

There is no dream in second chances
And you wasted yours and more
With all your emotional destruction
As you continue to cry for war.

But remove your gripping fingers
From my delicately manicured hand
You were hoping for understanding
But you've alienated everyone in the land.

Remember I hate everything you stand for

Remember I'm enemy number one
Keep that in mind when you're crying for my
approval
That in my world your tears raise the sun.

So pack up your lonely one man show
Time to take it on the road
I'll help carry your belongings to the station
This will be the happiest of all my loads.

We are done with you in our town
I'm sure another circus could use a clown.
Take a handkerchief to remember me by
And know that my life is looking up to know you're
down.

23. "Majesty"

The dawn came again,
    Crying.

Rising up over the mountain tops
And glaring at the sea.

It knows what happened
    Last night.

It could not see,
But that didn't prevent it from

Seeing
All those stars bathed in moonlight.

So many broken promises.

Trust

    has its own orbit.

24. "Promised And Sold"

Tell me again
How you didn't break my heart
How we're friends
How we're lovers
How you didn't tear my soul apart.

From those first moments of mistrust
I should have walked away
But I wanted to believe you
And so I stayed day after day.

Deep down I always knew
You were the one I could not trust
You always made it seem so easy
With your saccharin covered lust.

The moment there was another
I was Gone. I was Lost. I was Sold.
Given to another
To do as I was told.

You wanted me to say you treated me well

You want me to sing your praise
You want me to remember
Only happier, better days.

But when all I have left is deception
And when all you gave me to keep was pain
Just what am I supposed to remember
Except the days my tears fell hard like rain.

The smoke is on the horizon
The fire is in the house
Your dream, it seems, is over,
For I've woken up, and I've moved out.

25. "Hurricane Death"

62

There is lightening in the winter

there is softness in the sly

tempered talent with

unholyness

always

wondering

asking why

unbelievable this sadness

uncontrollable this rage

I stop to stand beside you

and my story gains a page

the storm whispers as it thunders

flashes of light and bells of pain

flooded fountains

running over

everything

silence falling

like a dream

unforeseeable this nausea

unquenchable this thirst to feel sane
I lay down among the rivers
yet my body does not age

this rain runs wild across the values
sweeping devastation o'er the plains
fierce flying
clouds of conscience
the gods
angry
in their reign

undeniable this flooding
unbeatable these tidal waves
I let the water carry may soul away
but my body stays where it lays

26. "How To Give Up: A Primer (Rough Draft)"

Slowly softly cry alone

Knowing no one else is listening

Knowing no one really cares

Knowing no one us coming for you

Knowing you can't save yourself

Let alone

Anyone else.

Seated alone at the dinner table

The food is cold

It doesn't matter

No one will notice but you

And you're too nauseous to eat.

Remember better times

Times when the dagger wasn't

Quite so deep in your side

When you were happy

Or so you thought

Or so you remembered

Or maybe not.

Quietly slow your breathing
Say it's because you are not well
Remember it's key they all think you're fine
Because you should be able to handle this
Because there's nothing you can't do
Because they need you to keep believing the lie
Because so do you.

Let those pieces of your soul slowly crumble
Like pieces of burnt paper barely intact
That paper, that contract, that dream,
Is over.

And as your memory turns to ash
Pour a tall glass of straight vodka
Mix the ashes of your soul in well
It might even be beautiful.

Slowly say the names over everyone that hurt you;
Sip. Cry. Repeat.
And
When the demons come again this time.
Don't resist.
Enlist.

27. "Flood Minutiae"

Like a bamboo fountain,

One drop,
Stop.

One drop,
Stop.

One drop,
Stop.

Like a bamboo fountain.

One drop,
The splash.

No longer able to contain the
Wall of tears.

No longer able to withhold
A stomach full of bile.

What was that last drop?

II. Blood

28. "Flicker"

Out of the night you step and cry
Not caring whether I do or die;
A zoetrope of men's actions over again
Repeating incessantly until the end.

How many times can you walk away
Me in tears begging you to stay;
Once more, crushing the heart of this dove,
Each time you abandon me in the name of love.

Your excuses are tired, just like my soul,
Whirling round and round a ten foot pole;
The moment comes when the rope is done in,
Springing me free after another violent run in.

The bruises don't show, but they're still there,
Carefully shielded by the flowers in my hair
My bleeding knees scabbed from earlier days,
Scars caught between beatings and kneeling to pray.

My Rosary is dedicated to you,
To your fists in the walls…your abandonment too;

Each tear a prayer for deliverance,

From the pain, the love, this unholy trance.

I walk alone night after night;

Screaming my rage like losing a fight;

I bathe in sorrow each day anew,

But when you need me, there's always a message

from you.

29. "Canopic"

Sometimes I walked
through your whispers
a wild wilderness
of head and heart

special circumstance
build of blood and blindness
contrived in tangles
of trials and starts

satin lined loneliness
turn from pieces frayed
a jar of dry tears
of whole pieces and devastated parts

30. "Monarch"

Unbalanced unbalances
I spit in the dust;
My heart a rigid bear trap
Covered in mistrust.

No room for patience
No room for peace;
No blanket suggestions
Not even a cup of coffee at least.

Parading your wares as she dances and sings
I am exhausted from flying;
She's looking for a flock to join
I have no air left in my wings.

I fly alone with special needs
A broken person always too real for the big reveal;
And as I peel the curtain back
It's just me alone, unable to feel.

31.”Blue, Period”

washing a thousand colors from my hair
each a shadow of memory
of a time I was somewhere

I turn and I look and I find that you're gone
your visit was a window
my heart just a pawn

you bathed me in promises you never could keep
popping bubbles like wishes
you gave me in your sleep

I can't say you left if you never were there
just temporary emotions
like the colors in my hair

32. "Marionette"

I want you to want me

cautious love born from twin hearts

I pull at your strings

peeling back the wrapper

trying to let you catch my eye

I want you to want me

bite by bite taking me in

I pull at your clothes

peeling back the wistful wonder

hoping you really see me this time

needing the burn of your rope

on my fingers

piece by pierce

you sing me to sleep

hoping I won't notice what your hands are really

doing

33. "For Noah"

Roiling in pain as you grip my voodoo doll tighter
Do you like the way it makes you feel?
Currents of false dominance coursing right through
you
At this point I think power is your only meal.

Gaunt and hollow and cold to the touch
the others, they think you have died
but I still feel your tightening grip
and I can see the fear and delight in your eyes.

But even though you cut me so deeply
and you hope to make me run from these men of
blood.
Clearly you've underestimated me; you can't really
see
that I'm just biding my time until my reign washes
you away in a flood.

34. "Velvet Seats"

You held my hand in the movies

once;
careful, tentative
wanting

to be sensitive
and caring
It was obvious
you hated it.

You.

Hated.

It.

I should have known then.

35. "Alone"

I.

Six weeks of silence
Eight days of second guessing
myself

I'm cold from crying
So afraid of what I've
become

I look to love
And end up
lost

II.

I can find my way
for fear of being hurt
again

When you left
you took my
heart

You broke me in pieces
And I cried until I
heaved

III.

You never said goodbye
I always wondered
why

Six weeks of silence
and still I
cry

36. "Tombstone Dreams"

What do I have to do

to convince you

I don't like you?

What do I have to say

to show you

for me this is no fun?

What do I have to do

to make you understand

how much I hate this?

What do I have to say

to pull your heart

out of your hand?

It's like you're living in a ghost town.

Its like you're living in a dream.

But for me it is a nightmare,

and I want to do

is scream.

37. "An Inch More To The Left"

I don't feel a victim
I don't feel sad
I just feel the numbness
of where my face met your hand

there's nothing you can say to me
there nothing I can scream
all I feel is emptiness
where once there was a dream

I long for what once might have been
I long for who you were
I long for something other than nothingness
I long for trust that doesn't burn

we lived a life a promises
we lived a life of pain
we lived a life of pretense
now it all just feels the same

I wonder when you made the choice
to put the knife into my flesh

I wonder when you realized

you were willing to bring me to my death

and sure I still yet live and breathe

and walk around just like I used to do

but underneath all the skin is scarred

and all because of you

38. "Abundance"

I wake up in tears
muscles sore
from wading through
the tar in your heart

each step like breaking through glass
ten thousand cuts from tiny shards
so much more painful
than my judgments

my blood splashed
across your face
you worry not in your emotional drought
saying you have tears to spare

39. "Third Act In Two Parts"

Part I.

I lay awake so full of hate
Seething at memories where I beg and scrape
I'm so badly burned I don't know where to turn
Quite divisiveness I have yet to learn.

I bleed at your hands each and every day
Some new scar emerges some enraged fresh pain
And you still live without consequence
Your conscience clear
No regrets.

So here we stand on cliff edges both
You've lied for ropes
I've lost all hope
And as our old friends rescue your soul
I'm left all alone
Searching for anything to make this pain dull.

Part II.

I hate you more than this lesson learned
Sometimes I long for the tables to be turned

For you to live in my heart of pain
So full of despair so full of disdain.

But you could never understand
What it meant to love
Your heart was bland
So you used me while it suited you so
And when you were done you didn't care if it
was my end.

I don't know if I'll ever be free
Of all this pain and treachery
Your harshness haunts me until this day
I wish you and this pain would finally go away.

40. "In Sickness I: Root Rot"

When I was born

I believed

in believing;

blue black bones,

bleeding hearts,

not deceiving.

I bled for you

blue blood and

red tears;

broken broken promises,

young love,

secret fears.

You told me that

you loved me

with each caressing blow;

a play by play of affection,

pay-per-view,

all a show

But woven amongst

broken promises

was the girl I used to be;

tried and true,

loyal to you,

and never one to lie, not me.

So what happens now

the tables are turned

the man behind the curtain

is exposed;

your love for the blond,

for more important

than the death of a rose.

41. "In Sickness II: Evidence Is A Vaccination For The Heart"

All the secrets and lies,
your good guy disguise,
the praises you didn't keep;
my broken heart,
my damaged dreams,
the way you made me weep.

I want to believe I wasn't a pawn,
I know it isn't true.
The lies I hear from former friends,
they all originate from you.
Of how I broke your heart, your world
when I walked out the door;
but that was lucky number seven months
that I endured, such hell,
before I couldn't take it anymore.

So as we play the game of blame
I have a message for your soul-
my aura, it has Polaroids,

of the bruises and stitches

you left during your starring role.

A simple reminder of life's blue truths,

that black eyes, they turn purple too.

Your cut scratched knuckles

a reference

to the fights the walls

had with you.

And while my skin remained unbroken,

as your promises faded away,

my heart broke daily – everyday the habitual ritual

while I wailed and begged you to stay.

In the end you chose your other life,

and chose to leave me behind;

broken and battered, but stronger, which matters,

for now I'm resistant to your lies.

42. "In Sickness III: Malady Not Contagious

I know that you abused me
used me, came and went as you saw fit,
and while I can barely speak of it
my blue soul apart was ripped.

While I was born I believed
in believing,
garnet red blood
across the stone.

I bled for you,
Perpetually,
until the day you ran away home.

For that was my true destruction,
your infidelities aside.
Just perpetual degradation
of my spirit,
my body your shield, your ride.

I don't believe you ever loved me,
no light in your darkness,

that's for sure;

But you should know that I really loved you,
and of that,
there is no cure.

43. "Custer At Heart"

Sing me a song of celebration
Of our family, of the land,
Sing of plastic beads and
Faux suede dream catchers
For that is all you understand.

Beg me again to be your one and only
Beg me again to pray with you
Then watch me burn the altar
Than betray the Gods that I pray to.

Our house was bathed in fire
Our home was packed in ice
An Oglala nightmare
Was my recurring sacrifice.

I was never blood of your blood
I was never your sister in Christ
I was a girl that needed guidance
Not lies upon lies upon lies.

I pray my rosary for another

I know you exist and its enough
To keep my distance from the hearth
To be like Caine and roam the Earth.

The drums call out the warriors
The women sing as much as they cry
And you pretend to be one of each
Telling of how you've lived and died.

I wander listless among ruins
My identity shattered mirrors at best
And still you cry out for my affection
Turning me to stone like all the rest.

I never meant to abandon you
I said goodbye as I left
But you broke my treaties and stole my land
Memories set afire and set adrift.

We can whisper of tomorrow
We can cry out for the past
But boundaries are sacred
And you have crossed your last.

44. "Nomad? No, Mad."

She walked slowly through the desert
Hands caressing cacti as if they were silks
The dust swirled in her footsteps
As she looked for you.

Bleeding out of both eyes
Clothes torn and stained
Feet nearly broken from walking the earth
As she looked for you.

Carefully she calls out your true name
This is why she knows you are hiding
For only powerful magic or deceit can cloak
As she looked for you.

Hiding in some hole in the rock
In the arms of some one else's broken heart
You smell the sweet grass and the sage as she burns
As she looked for you.

Hands made of quartz and turquoise
All those dreams were made on stars which

Fell to the ground
When she stopped looking for you.

Only then did you realize
Only then did you care
That it was her oxygen keeping you alive
When she stopped looking for you.

And as you sputtered and coughed
And as you begged and pleaded
She found you by a dying fire
When she stopped looking for you.

She wouldn't hold your hand
Preferring the sting of the cholla
Than to giving her last blood to your dying body.
That's why she stopped looking for you.

45. "Armistice Elusive"

Tell me again about your sacrifice
Tell me how you move and parry
Tell me how you're fighting this war

Single-Handedly
Both sides
No winners
The only loser, me.

Why do we wander
Smoothing our skirts and pretending
Everything is alright.

I thought there was a reason
I thought you meant to stay
I thought this wasn't an offensive
How could I be so wrong?

Unlimited leaving and whispered stares
Climbing social ladders rung by rung
In fishnets and stiletto heels

Whip at my back, stars in my eyes
Colorblock transitions grinding to a halt
As I catch the look of your heart.

Standard issue combative emotions
Peace rung out and hung up to dry
Careful consideration of each word

Still a dice roll to see if you'll believe me
Careful patient knife to the throat if not
Sweet assassin surrender
Maybe one day we'll put down our guns.

46. "Domestic Violence"

She believed you when you promised
She believed you when you lied
All your heart string guns blazing
As she sat at home and cried

Do you remember screaming
As she stood upon the stairs
Pushing her down when she was broken
And then proceeded with your affair

She hid alone in the darkened closet
The smallest place that she could find
Hiding from all the words and more the punches
That would surely fill your mind

She fled with out ever truly leaving
Always afraid of it getting worse
Meanwhile you bullied her at every turn
While helping yourself to the wallet in her purse

She would have given you everything always
She would have always made you first

But you chose to demean and destroy her
An abusive vampire looking to slake his thirst.

47. "Suffocated"

She shifted softly in the sunlight
There was no end to her dream
Wild warm oblivion
There wasn't much else she could say

Comprised of caring and cariño
She too longed for him
But like the night
He was long gone

Special circumstance and secret rituals
He had led her down the path
And now she lay waiting
For her own strangler

There wasn't anything to be done
But believe
In the wide warmth obliviating her
As she slowly faded into memory.

48. "Burn The Witch"

That feeling of slow pain
Of having a hope and a dream
And of having your wishes squeezed from it
Like the most bitter lemon

Your hands bruised from holding on so tightly
Your wrists bruised from the ropes holding you in
place
No sense
No surrender
Just silence as the snow falls, obscuring your tears.

That cold ice christening
Reborn into darkness
Poison slowly seeping into your subconscious
There is no hope in hell
There is nothing but shallow despair

Sainted surrender seems possible now
Letting the beatings happen without discontentment
Some sort of consensual pain of consequence
Each day a little closer, now, to death.

I love the hope of your surrender

I dare to dream of no more pain.

But I know all of that is fantasy

As I go slowly quietly insane

I wish for solace in the sunlight

I beg for freedom from the cold

The patience in my heart grows weary

As you convince me I will never win

I keep caressing all the open wounds

Watching as the blood trickles softly down

I keep from crying just almost barely

My true voice has lost its sound

And in reflection I am nothing

Just another soul to sell

I was broken for your pleasure

Now live or die, this is my hell.

49. "What Is Unspoken In A Support Group"

There was something
Unfortunate
To sitting in mixed silence.

Large groups
Decomposing into small
Visits without
Much disregard
For much other

Than each's
Own interest.

50. "Home Or Misplaced Self-Worth"

I used to believe
In transformation
Long lipped in my desire to mold
The decaying world into a budding
Flower of hope
This was a time of
Absolute need.

What did I achieve?

Everything.

Moving incessantly toward
Purity-goodness
As sad desperate soul bathed
In rays
Of faith
Clothed in love
I began to strip
Away the pain.

Dark deceptive betrayal

A secret consuming

Guilt

Self-bathing

Feeding on denial

And disgust.

There was no place for

Happiness then

This was a place

Of self-depreciation

Of secret hope for hope

Of absolute hidden confusion.

51. "April 3rd, 2013, 11:23am"

I believed in you
Of dreams
And love
And pretty things

I thought you loved me
But you don't
You cant be bothered
To care
To ask.

You sound so cheerful on the phone.
How is your girlfriend?

52. "The Sanctity Of Street Light Confessions"

I always believe you when you're lying
Lying softly, lying hard
Careful construction of the fantasy
Uncultured whispered, untoward found;

I'd like to believe that you weren't lying
Telling truths over telling tails
Of considerably large fishnets and cocks
Careful shoes, careful clocks;

I know that wishes are wasteful
But these aren't and more they're dreams
Yet I find myself tired of writing
No more rivers, no more streams.

…

I don't want to tell your story anymore
I'm sick of being broken
And all of your pain
Of all that unending need, full of hate, from your
brain;

Somehow I'm caught
In the loop you made me
Looks of crazy
Lochs of tears;

Crystalline terror filling my heart
My head my blood curdling with each new start
And bathed in anxiety through and through
I'm sick of everything, everything about you.

53. "Cyanide"

Untold transition
trapped with taint,
I can't help but feel poisoned.

Too much too fast
the drugs are quick,
I can't help but begin to cry.

Full tilt enlightenment
catching my breath,
I can't help but crawl home.

Crafted self destruction
you pull me tight against you,
tasting the toxin on my lips.

And you smile
you always did like drugs,
no matter the cost.

54. "Ivory Labyrinth"

I follow the ghost trails

of our lost life;

of magic moments long forgotten

rekindled amongst strife.

You didn't mean to walk away

and leave my crying behind;

but now you've gotten to where you

were going to;

and realized

you're no longer alive.

I follow the ghost whispers

of our hearts broken and torn;

of the world we knew,

of a life we lived until worn.

You didn't mean to disappear

and leave your beloved so unkind;

burdened in pain,

soul looking for happiness broken and blind;

so I wander lost in memories,

knowing I may be looking for you enshrined;

but I'll only ever find remnants of

the body you maligned.

55. "Quietly In Prayer"

I close my eyes but don't see ball rooms
we never married in my head,
we just lay in purple splendor
eternally alone, safe in my bed.

Your world mapped like a catechism
having to know the right path to get around,
to move from one city to the next
and not get caught nailed to the ground.

I always thought you'd make me happy
even when you made me sad,
and sometimes I can't help but miss you
when tears and tears are all I had.

I don't wonder what you're doing
its all there for me to see,
the other path I could have taken
the secret life you had with me.

56. "Consubstantiation"

Fingering
The last drop of heartbreak
Letting it spill over
And run down my luscious curves

Those things you said
Fat, unattractive, undesirable
Rolling down my rolls

As the weight fades off me
All your self-hate imprints
Telling me I am ugly

But you are uglier
In your hate and self-loathing
The worst library to borrow from

You can have it back
As I surrender
To self love and resurrection

Warm sins as I remember

My heart didn't shatter
Your hammer did.

57. "Reflections"

Spider webs on fractured glass

Slow moving fragments slowly pass

Ships in the night

As emotions curl and twirl

Following the patterns of my broken mind

Streets free from sanity

Roads to nowhere

Just broken pieces bleeding me dry

Unpopulated cities can't handle people

Yet there they are

And move in tandem

Walking the fine lines of civility

Believing in Jesus and justice

Driving their cars down silken threads

No signs no stops

Just accidents over and over again

Darker dystopia entitled twists

Exhausted monsters done with nice

All we need now are mirrors and dreams

But here nothing is what it seems

Spider webs on fractured glass

So moving fragments slowly pass

No signs no stops

Into the night

58. "I Dream Of Pawn Shops"

The facets rise frightened from diamonds sparking in
the sunlight,
Thick with the blood from which they were forged;
All hammers and nails and curls and lies; nothing
feeling right,
Memorial fires burning, emotional ore once again re-
poured.

You gave me jewels as a voiceless bribe,
You bathed me in gold to make me stay;
Your offering to the old dead gods,
Just made me feel like you were predator, and I was
prey.

Unholy matrimony plays over in my head,
Knowing everything was wrong;
Feeling narcissistic deception seeping from your
pores,
Why couldn't I ever ring the alarm?

A repeated pattern in my life,
As I'm used and publicly thrown away;

Each hand wanting to help me recover,
Just the same lies as every other day.

So my rings they sparkle and they shine,
I wear them daily so you don't whine;
But I know they are just shackles and chains,
My constant jail made of 18 carat pain.

59. "Best Friends, Once Removed"

Didn't you wonder about my silence
Was your garrote to my throat a good enough clue
Was I belligerently bleeding
Were my tears an annoyance
Sorry, am I bothering you?

Overjoyed and undersold I remember being hand in
hand
We felt blood run through our fingers like particles of
sand
I smiled as you turned me black and blue
The bruises I hid every moment I was with you
Breaking bones not quite yet executed through.

In your arms I believed I was meant for endless death
Idyllic incantations woven into each and every word
you spoke
Holding me close/Holding me hostage
No way to become free, as you squeezed and bled me
broke.

My heart was always broken and even my womb

knew
Do you remember how you denied me through and
through and through
Not your ideal you said / my body was your problem
So so much cruelness, never knowing which way
Your anger was going to go.

Burning candles, burning flesh, burning roses,
begging for death, preparing for the last.
Handcuffed to your future as you longed for your
past,
Imagining successes and failures held all the gravitas;
And surrounded by minions who loved your world
They were all happy to watch me burn; they never
said a word.

Didn't I wonder about their silence as you held
A knife to my throat?
Was I not crying loud enough;
Was my pleading pain not what they wanted to see in
their fantasy?
Blank slate boilerplate perfect couple can't possibly be
in ruins.
But this wasn't what we wrote.

"Am I bothering you all?," I ask.

My silence done and gone.

You ask me to keep quiet still, the pain too much you

plea;

But I don't answer to your desires anymore,

No matter now,

Goodbye,

I'm free.

BLUE BONES, BLOOD ROSES, BLACK EYES

III. Black

60. "Opening Night"

Spotlight on your narcissism
blind black feeling caged,
wanting to scream frustration
but my frustration will not age.

For you can solely see you
you are oblivious to my pain,
and hearing your name in rage ragged screaming
is just as good as hearing your name on a stage.

I just want to cry and cry
burning desire to curl up, lay down, and die,
though really I wish I could fly,
but you've clipped my wings with all your lies.

And there you sit smiling
looking concerned when the need does arise,
best make sure everyone sees that tear, you wouldn't
want to have to reprise,
plus it's important the right people see you cry.

It doesn't matter what happens to those around you

Nero playing fiddle while all of Rome falls,

but one day you will crumble

and no one will be there to take your calls.

The lights they dim softly for my one woman show

the audience is assembled, full of people you know;

by now you've realized your error, seen the playbills

in ink,

all I have to say is "no more keeping quiet, better

make yourself a drink."

61. "In Your Hands"

I dreamed of you last night
watching you walk through my day;
curled in patient broken bones
and bleeding from the broken heart burned black
skewered a fresh new way.

I feel like everything shattered as we went to prayer
hand stitching rips instead of being present in the
faith;
crawling slowly back up to my dreams of sanctity
and hoping life will one day be what it seems and not
this wraith.

So take my hand and dry my eyes
free me truly from your spell and
bring me to heel with place and time;
save my blackened bleeding heart from its hell
deliver me from thus the unforgiving life that is mine.

62. "Light Years Away"

My heart is like an open pomegranate
Cracked open for all the world to see;
Each seed a secret feeling or emotion
Being devoured by everyone but me.

My heart just hurts and cries inside
Like pins and needles were used too many times;
And this brick broken inside my chest
Overwhelms me with anxiety and I just feel less and
less as feeling dies.

Chest like a black hole
So full and yes such emptiness, enveloping me in an
asteroid field;
Spinning me sideways into oblivion as I desperately
cling to what's around me
Argument and anger, fists and words the weapons
that you wield.

I burn and bleed, alone, no mercy,
And cracked hands hold onto slippery poles;
Others try to hold onto me but I am already too far

into the ether, Or they fear to let go of their own
roles.

Lost in the pull of my own elongated heart
Lost in the fruit of the bed that I never made;
This black hole of endless nothingness
So much better than if you stayed.

63. "Deliver Me From Evil"

I feel like I changed to make you happy
And now I am being punished for it.

Devastated that she and I are alike in any way,
You tell me this pain is my own fault.

Some moments I wonder - am I just
Going to completely lose it.

Have I lost it already?
Tell me again how I'm wrong?

Feeling sick from the inside out.

Making sacrifice after sacrifice for you,
While you didn't even notice.

Feeling hollow living alone
In the house we built
Together.

You say you don't need me anymore.

Yet the ghost of you is here with me
Everywhere
I turn.

Night after night of the living dead in my living
room.

Does anyone know an exorcist?

64. "Taxidermy"

There in the whispered corner

Shadowed in symphony

Covered in tears

I live to breathe

At your permission

Uncomfortable silences

Uncontrollable fears

There is no fabled fairytale ending

Just controlled carrion

Sabotaged over years

I wish to wonder

What became of me

Shot in the glade

Mounted with cheers

There isn't a moment

I can forget this

Scars too visible

Pain too great

I can remember

To walk stoically

Unflinching stare

Unaccepting of defeat

65. "How To Survive His Fist: A Guide"

Be one with the pain
Blossoming across your face
Breathing heavy
Desperate tears arrive in force.

Twisting hands
Wringing themselves over and over
Bleeding hangnails
I've pulled off to keep breathing.

Closed fist
Exploding next to me
Crying out
For the wall to hit back this time.

This isn't the reason
I feel you abused me;

Your lips
Always saying
I wasn't good enough

Was.

66 (6). "Valkyrie"

My insanity rides in victory
Our disagreements loud and clear
Unfortunate turn of events you say
Just calm down, don't interfere

I am too soft you say, all candy
Too weak, always sick at home
I'm not discreet about bleeding from my wherever
As a lady I should have never let you know

I'm too refined for your porn start fantasies
Buttons on my Victorian collar lace up too high
Not blonde enough, not pale enough
Personal sins of the literal flesh on my head and
thighs

Do you remember saying I was worthless
As I tore my shirt to shreds
As you watched my sense of self self-destruct
While you texted her about your day from the side of
my bed

You put in my head that it was always my fault
Everything including the dishes and sex told you I
didn't belong
Do you remember punching the wall beside me
Accusing me when you were wrong

There was the day that we lost power
And you screamed me into tears
Blaming me for being useless
That I should be on my knees begging out of fear

Bored with the virgin, needing a whore
You pushed me out of my house and locked the door
Now I see ghosts of her face around town
This new girl you say, is better than me, your former
sad clown

You don't want me, you never did
But I should be happy in this new reality
You'll still be my friend you say with glee
Even more I can make when I take out us three

A better thought you had for me
You and she will move in; we'll live happily
I'll pay the rent and hide in my room

You'll try to be quiet when you tell her not tonight,
and it's you.

Shattered and shaken and living a lie
You left me for something you hated
Constantly quieting my mind as you shattered it
again
Telling me I'm a coward, and paranoid for not
        wanting to see you again.

The ongoing saga of me, the fool
I don't know how to feel or what is real
Onlookers pointing and staring as I cry in the street
My body withering away as I am unable to eat.

No sleep no dreams, no whispers of love
Just nightmares of you and murdered doves
Constantly nauseous in the new life
This my new title, your ex-wife.

Still overwhelmed and feeling alone
Tonight you are in her bed, and I cry tears of stone
I am old news to you, dead weight, a bother,
I'm not the former love of your life; I'm just your
starter

You can't see me, my heart, my broken mind
My insanity holding a ticker tape parade as I go blind
The pain so strong, the constant pain
Only needles and straps will keep me sane

My love, my trust, my sense of self
Stepping stones for your 9th level Dark Elf
I am alone now, make no mistake
Six feet underground without a wake

And it breaks my heart that you don't care
But that's the nature of your power, I hid and
cowered
This is the way you abused me
To live in fear of your unending glower

You literally made me sick and I nearly died
I vomited blood, I cried and cried
You broke my heart, you broke my mind
But I survived, I even thrived.

For though you hoped I would fade away
I stand strong and tall, my scars full of things to say
And despite your constant emotional torture and pain

I'm living the life you wanted, and I hope that it's
driving you slowly, delicately, and deliberately insane.

67. "Liar"

I have never felt this bad in my whole life.

My heart,
Broken.

My spirit,
Weak.

My body,
Desiccated.

My mind
Lost.

My dream,
Snatched away.

My world,
Given handily to another.

Tell me again why you seek to humiliate me.

Maybe this time I'll understand.

Maybe this time I'll believe you when you tell me it's my fault.

68. "Huntsman"

I remember when
You stole my whispers
I remember when
You made me cry
Softly gently
Full of destruction
And me begging
Asking why?

Unholy order
Unopened dream
Black bruises blossoming
Each and every eve
And there you practice
Holding court
Masturbating your ego
Your favorite sport;
For me, never any reprieve.

I'll always doubt
If you really loved me
I'll always question

If you cared

What would have happened

If I hadn't begged you

Would you have carved out my heart

Or had it spared?

69. "Madonna"

I wake from a savage dream,
And still I'm trapped in your anger all the same.
Why do you seek my destruction?
Why do you harbor all this pain?

You see me merely as some whore,
Just banging at your door, again and again,
When really I sit quietly,
Just waiting for you to go insane…

Have you ever once considered
That this isn't about you,
That until you started firing, the war was inside your
head,
And that I was traveling softly, so as to not to leave a
tread?

No. And though you salt the earth as your home
slowly catches fire
All you see is your own face,
In your bubble, in your space;
Without a care if the rest burns to the ground around

you…nothing left but dark desire.

You wonder if I see you
Windows always open just for me but "taking in the
open air;"
The hear you gave long ago gone,
As you desperately seek some sort of spare

Your tears they fall on deaf ears now,
I do not have any pity nor semblance of care;
You buried my concern in concrete years ago,
This one is for [----].

70. "Vietcong"

I want to believe in your persistence
As you plead with me to stay;
But my tears are falling faster
Than I know how to say.

Your constant caring kindness
When it suits the gallery;
But revelations of addiction
Are saved especially for me.

My skin remains unblemished
But my face feels black and blue;
A cacophony of harassment in my heart
And it's forever thanks to you.

When you asked me to be with you
It seem like tropical paradise to be;
But the forests were peppered with landmines
Hand planted among the flowers,
Deliberately hidden from me.

Each ordinance handcrafted, artisanal, bespoke,

Cascading blasts all down my ribcage, my lungs
billowing with smoke;
Bathed in oils and salves and potions, so that there
would be no telling scars,
It's a secret that bleeds blood for tears,
Always and forever engaged in your pretty, petty
wars.

71. "She Waits"

Seeping sadness
smoke curls through memory
caught in my hair awash in the wind;
my eyes try to dance for you,
but we each pull away
before we can begin.

Stepping forward into nothingness
blackened hearts charred and cracked;
seeping sadness made from memory
I look to you to love,
but death is vast.

Walk with me under the flowered gate
away from darkness of the past;
let wind wash smoke curled in memory,
let dead hopes die
and turn to ash.

Seeping sadness I try to cry and look back for you
to look to love instead of hesitate;
but seeping sadness stands its ground tonight

Again this night our twin-souled ships

will simply pass with baited breath of love too late.

72. "Dusk"

It's like I keep waiting for winter,
For the tide to set in;
For what little joy to be shuttered,
For the end to begin.

I can't help but feel alone,
Despite the fact we walk side by side;
Holding hands amidst the apocalypse,
A setting sun across the sand.

Spilling secrets beneath whispered sentiments,
I turn and call your ahem into the wind;
Bruised and battered our souls meet one last time,
Coming together to let the end begin.

73. "She Took Cash At The Door"

My hands in front of me
begging you to stop-
volley after volley-
you shelled me with pain,
but as I begged for mercy
her vengeance grew vain.

Do you even remember her name?

74. "40 Days"

I: Genesis

> Your desert is a deserted place
> and I traveled there for years,
> I had thought I had a home there
>
> *but you destroyed it with your fears.*

II: Exodus

> A sledgehammer to our family life
> as you broke apart our vows,
> civilian casualty hype enough
>
> *I need a place for the bodies to be housed.*

III: Leviticus

> And as the sun beat down upon
> your barren wasted skin,

you hold up your tattoos as trophies

proclaiming some sort of sick distorted win.

IV: Numbers

And I lived homeless in your valley
trying desperately to make you see,
that we could rebuild anywhere together

but it would take both of us not only me.

V: Deuteronomy

But you left the angels for the saints
not realizing you had lost your way,
reveling in your degradation

and pitying me in my desire to stay.

VI: The New Testament

But still I wandered your desert dream
until I knew for sure you had gone,
for I refused to abandon you

for, unlike you, I knew it was wrong.

75. "Crematorium"

And then I cry
And blindly burn
Ashes coating my skin

Tired and toiled
I fill my urn
Ashes end and begin

And here you sing
Sad song eulogies
Where you pretend no sin

And then I cry
I've burned and died
And you promote the legend of your win

76. "M.A.D. - Mutually Assured Destruction"

I remember that feeling
of losing control
where the rules changed
day by day

And you sat serenely
savoring the pain
as you toyed with my heart
September through May

I didn't believe you could
be so cruel
shattering my heart and mind
and soul

And so you won
destroying me
and scattering the pieces
even then making me pay your bill

And in the end
as tears broke hearts

you tore me down

into tiny shreds and false starts

And I lost control

of mind and soul

I wonder which one of us more

I wished was dead, a knife through the heart

77. "Plastered"

I remember not touching you.
Back when I was beautiful.
Back when you pretended to want me.
Back before you broke my heart.

Sleeping broken I woke alone.
Buried in sand surrounded by stones.
There aren't any wings, there aren't any prayers.
There's only me beneath these Filo dough layers.

There were concrete floors and mirrored halls.
There were champagne sinks and bleeding walls.
There was nothing I could say or do.
When you decided I was done with you.

Painful steps down stair after stair.
Past nuclear waste amid noxious air.
Beholden to nothing but shadows of the past.
Nothing to hope for as I sit long in my cast.

78. "Tomorrow"

Tell me again how it's all ok
How it's not really happening
Not in the way I say

You say I got my culture from a video
Bitch please - What is it you think you know?

Worn and tired my constitution is
Ruined, ragged; just bag it

Isn't that what you wanted though?
Me without agency, celebrating you, the hero?

White and upper class polishing that silver spoon...
(You know the neighbors like to look at it – they'll be
'round soon)

But I wouldn't know; I've not met them
Not since you built this wall I'm paying for, cut my
blossom from its stem.

So you've got your white and your blue, your
something old and something new, but what about
Red?
The way I learned no blood pumps through those
veins, the true you.

So tell me again how this is best for my life
why your choices are better than mine, this inherent
strife.
How it'll all/never happen; when, when, and how you
say.
Don't worry I'll still kneel at your altar and pray.

But only for one more day.

79. "Center Ring"

An angry empty circus

at your mercy sir,

cold and dark

but the lights are on outside.

I turn to see you

but there's nothing there but shadows,

splintered and tired

walk alone must I.

I meant to leave

when you left me,

yet I'm still here

spiraling slowly into an invisible black hole.

Stretched so thin

I could be mistaken for a shadow myself,

underneath a tent of shame

my pain a costume of closed eyes.

To turn around and look at you

my heart full of pain,

to look at you

and to say everything that I need saying,

An angry empty circus

at your mercy sir,

no hope no spark

but the lights are on outside.

80. "Crushed"

and therein lies the rub

for when I dream

or when I dance,

for nothing I see matters to you

all you do is blindly prance

and as I wither slowly suffering

watching you look and look away,

I keep pretending that you care for me

for all I can do is stay

and once I'm dried on the vine

and dead to all

your mission is complete

to have everything you could take from me

and run away on coward's feet

81. "Left Behind / Genesis"

There is no happiness in freedom
When your bonds have been tied too tight
Just a tingling in your limbs
Who used to remember how to fight

Now the ropes are gone, the shackles too
And you're left feeling confused
For you felt that all that existed was
His abusive attention toward you

You remember how he looked at you
His eyes deeply full of hate and blame
As he remade his world around him
And your dungeon stayed the same.

What's to be done with is new freedom
Eyes adjusting to the light
Where do you even go from here
When there's no one you have to fight.

You ride the train in simple silence

Watch the countryside go by
You weep at the loss of your reality
Though if you'd stayed you would have died

At the station there's a taxi
And a suitcase full of clothes
You'll look better free of handcuffs
They were never something you chose

In the bathroom as you button
A pink Chanel tweed suit
You beg the world for mercy
As they expect to meet the real you

You wonder what he's doing
If he's still abusive or in pain
If he has a new slave to disappoint him
Someone new to hide the bruises and the shame

You step out into the sunlight
Blinking back the tears and sun
There may be no happiness in freedom
But it was happily hard fought and won.

A NOTE ON SURVIVING

I appreciate that the contents of this book are painful. They were painful to live, they were painful to write, and they have been painful to process. I would also like to acknowledge all the stories of pain and survival that friends and family have shared with me, creating our shared experience. Thank you for always being honest and helping me recover from the trauma of my past. It really does get better.

If you are currently in an abusive relationship, know that it is not your fault. Tell someone. Tell everyone. Your friends and family want to help. One of my only regrets was not being honest with those closest to me, and not asking for help sooner. There is no shame in honesty. There is no shame in therapy.

If you need guidance call:

National Domestic Violence Hotline

1.800.799.7233 | www.ndvh.org

ACKNOWLEDGMENTS

Many thanks to Phil Gevaux for all of his love, kindness, and support. To my parents, Ann Nadine Sánchez and Joseph Marcus Sánchez – love you.

Also to all the members of my family who have been so support of my writing, thank you, thank you, thank you. Especially to my Uncle James, who bought the first copy I sold of <u>Hearts Aflame, Still Burning</u> – I was paying attention, and I love you too.

For reading this first and offering edits and praise, thanks to: Alysha Cohen, Angela Owens, Charles Orlando, Nicholas Ryan Howard, and Scott Lobdell.

For all your love, friendship, & support, thank you to: Osian Barnes, Kim Bertho, Leticia Bevilaqua, Sr. Colleen Braun, Fran Brennan and Al Faer, Deb Carfora, Fr. Nathan Castle, Leon Duah, Michael Duah, Mystie Erb, Ray Estrada, Damon and Jila Field, Sarah & Jonatan Funtowicz, Rob Gaudio and Janene Zakrajek, Jake and Fiona Hoban, Roxanna Huyghe, Nevena Jancovic, Roger Jarvis, Amy Lim, Jen Mayer, Mark Meloccaro, Tricia Milam, Paula Mirabal, Emma Morris, Margaret Murray, Angela O'Brien, Ashley and Ed Perridge, Natasha and Jim Radford, Simone

Silvestroni and Silvia Maggi, Shauna Stacy, Drew Sullivan, Matt Vanderschans, and Shelley Winegarner.

I would also like to thank my my Aunts Cesi, Cindy, Debra, Elizabeth, Geralynn, Katherine, Kres, Jane, Jean, Neela, Rebecca, and Theresa – as well as my Great Aunt Ida and Great Aunt Lou for their guidance in life. Also love to my Uncles Chris, John, Johnny, Juan, Rick, Rudy, Paul, Steve, Ted, and Tom for all of their love and support.

To my godparents Francine & David, thank you for everything. To Margaret for her kindness, always. To my cousins Anita, Anne, Anna, Asa, Anthony, Danielle, Cameron, Carmen, Carrie, Carlos, Chiefo, Jake, John, Katie, Kohl, Sara, Millie, Maya, Rachel, Randy, Tony, Woods, and Wyatt as well as Mario & Charles, Joe and Jenny, Patti, Patrizia, Paula, y todo la Familia– I love our shared stories, lets make more of them together. To Alysha, Gregg, & Eva thank you for sharing your love & home with me.
And to my brother Xoco, I'm happy to be your sister.

I would also like to thank the Gevaux family for being so supportive and welcoming. David and Irene – I am so honored to be joining the family. Thank you for being so loving. Dave and Tim – xo.
Millie and Hettie – Love you mucho.

To the Memory of Roy and Nadine, Eusebio and Cora, Mary Kressin, Aunt Mary, Aunt Rose, Joshua Littlewolf, and Paul Zuzich – thank you guiding me with your spirit.

Lastly, I would like to thank Irene Marston. She was a fierce woman, an incredible lady, and a role model of the highest order.
Love you Nan – may you Rest in Peace.

ABOUT THE AUTHOR

Rosa Nadine Xochimilco Sánchez was born from a blend of prairie wind, smudge sticks, and blue corn enchiladas; and her sensibilities leave her bridging culture, language, space, and spirit; always guided by all of her relations. She has been writing poetry since she was four years old, and has been publishing and performing her work throughout her life. She splits her time between Los Angeles, California, and London, England with her fiancé Phil, and her trusty mutt, Tubby – always in search of adventure and truth in love – not to mention quality cream tea spots and excellent taco trucks. You will most likely find her wandering the halls of the British Museum, tending to her garden, or hunting for used books in a charity shop.

This is Ms. Sanchez's second book of poetry, following her inaugural full-length publication of <u>Hearts Aflame, Still Burning</u>. She is currently working on a collection of essays about life in her family.